The Pocket Bible
On Faith

Scriptures to Renew Your Mind
and Change Your Life

Harrison House
Tulsa, Oklahoma

Unless otherwise indicated, all Scripture quotations are taken from the *King James Version* of the Bible.

07 06 05 04 03   10 9 8 7 6 5 4 3 2 1

The Pocket Bible on Faith—
Scriptures to Renew Your Mind and Change Your Life
ISBN 1-57794-592-1 (Formerly ISBN 0-89274-833-8)
Copyright © 1995, 2003 by Harrison House, Inc.
P.O. Box 35035
Tulsa, OK 74153

Introduction

Paul describes the spirit of faith in 2 Corinthians 4:13 as *believing* and *speaking* God's Word: "It is written: 'I *believed;* and therefore I have spoken.' With that same spirit of faith we also believe and therefore speak" (NIV).

Faith is *believing* and *speaking* what God says in the face of natural circumstances, reports, or diagnoses. Faith is putting agreement with the higher report of God's Word. God will not change His mind about the promises of His Word. They will become a reality in the life of the person who is willing to believe and speak His Word as the highest standard of truth.

To put agreement with God's Word in the face of sickness or disease, faith believes and speaks, "By Jesus' stripes I am healed." (Isaiah 53:5; 1 Peter 2:24.) In the face of mental torment, faith believes and speaks, "I have perfect peace because my mind is focused on the Lord." (Isaiah 26:3.) "I am far from oppression, and fear and terror will not come near me." (Isaiah 54:14.) In the face of lack, faith believes and speaks, "God supplies my every need according to His riches in glory by Christ Jesus." (Philippians 4:19.) "God's blessings make me rich, and He adds no sorrow with it." (Proverbs 10:22.) In the face of anxiety, faith believes and speaks, "I cast every care, worry, and anxiety upon the Lord." (1 Peter 5:7.)

The Pocket Bible on Faith contains examples which you can follow of faith in action from biblical accounts in both the Old and New Testaments. You will rise to a new level as you meditate upon the principles of faith presented in the Scriptures contained in this Pocket Bible. As a result, you will be better equipped to whip *every* challenge and overcome *every* hurdle, regardless of its complexity.

Because of the input of these power-packed, resurrection words, life will flow from your heart out through your lips. New heights and new victories—both spiritually and naturally—will be yours!

Prayer

Father, thank You for Your Word which is infused with the resurrection life of Your Son, Jesus.

As I take daily doses of the spiritual faith food contained in this Pocket Bible, help me to rise to a new level of victory, triumph, abundant joy, and prosperity of spirit, soul, and body.

Thank You, Holy Spirit, for quickening my eyes to see as Jesus sees; to hear as Jesus hears; to discern as He discerns; to speak as He speaks; to love as He loves; to be immovable in the face of any challenge, fully confident that God's Word will prevail.

Help me to imitate You accurately, Lord Jesus, in my every thought, word, and action. Transform me into a faith-filled champion, just as You are (1 John 4:17), in Your name I pray. Amen.

Faith Scriptures

Old Testament

And he [Abram] believed in the Lord; and he counted it to him for righteousness.

Genesis 15:6

And when Abram was ninety years old and nine, the Lord appeared to Abram, and said unto him, I am the Almighty God; walk before me, and be thou perfect.

And I will make my covenant between me and thee, and will multiply thee exceedingly.

And Abram fell on his face: and God talked with him, saying,

As for me, behold, my covenant is with thee, and thou shalt be a father of many nations.

Neither shall thy name any more be called Abram, but thy name shall be Abraham; for a father of many nations have I made thee.

And I will make thee exceeding fruitful, and I will make nations of thee, and kings shall come out of thee.

And I will establish my covenant between me and thee and thy seed after thee in their generations for an everlasting covenant, to be a God unto thee, and to thy seed after thee.

And I will give unto thee, and to thy seed after thee, the land wherein thou art a stranger, all the land of Canaan, for an everlasting possession; and I will be their God.

And God said unto Abraham, Thou shalt keep my covenant therefore, thou, and thy seed after thee in their generations.

Genesis 17:1-9

Therefore know that the Lord your God, He is God, the faithful God who keeps covenant and mercy for a thousand generations with those who love Him and keep His commandments.

Deuteronomy 7:9 NKJV

Now Jericho was securely shut up because of the children of Israel; none went out, and none came in.

And the Lord said to Joshua: "See! I have given Jericho into your hand, its king, and the mighty men of valor.

"You shall march around the city, all you men of war; you shall go all around the city once. This you shall do six days.

"And seven priests shall bear seven trumpets of rams' horns before the ark. But the seventh day you shall march around the city seven times, and the priests shall blow the trumpets.

"It shall come to pass, when they make a long blast with the ram's horn, and when you hear the sound of the trumpet, that all the people shall shout with a great shout; then the wall of the city will fall down flat. And the people shall go up every man straight before him"

Then Joshua the son of Nun called the priests and said to them, "Take up the ark of the covenant, and let seven priests bear seven trumpets of rams' horns before the ark of the Lord."

And he said to the people, "Proceed, and march around the city, and let him who is armed advance before the ark of the Lord."

So it was, when Joshua had spoken to the people, that the seven priests bearing the seven trumpets of rams' horns before the Lord advanced and blew the trumpets, and the ark of the covenant of the Lord followed them.

The armed men went before the priests who blew the trumpets, and the rear guard came after the ark, while the priests continued blowing the trumpets.

Now Joshua had commanded the people, saying, "You shall not shout or make any noise with your voice, nor shall a word proceed out of your mouth, until the day I say to you, 'Shout!' Then you shall shout."

So he had the ark of the Lord circle the city, going around it once. Then they came into the camp and lodged in the camp.

And Joshua rose early in the morning, and the priests took up the ark of the Lord.

Then seven priests bearing seven trumpets of rams' horns before the ark of the Lord went on continually and blew with the trumpets. And the armed men went before them. But the rear guard came after the ark of the Lord, while the priests continued blowing the trumpets.

And the second day they marched around the city once and returned to the camp. So they did six days.

But it came to pass on the seventh day that they rose early, about the dawning of the day, and marched around the city seven times in the same manner. On that day only they marched around the city seven times.

And the seventh time it happened, when the priests blew the trumpets, that Joshua said to the people: "Shout, for the Lord has given you the city!

"Now the city shall be doomed by the Lord to destruction, it and all who are in it. Only Rahab the harlot shall live, she and all who are with her in the house, because she hid the messengers that we sent.

"And you, by all means abstain from the accursed things, lest you become accursed when you take of the accursed things, and make the camp of Israel a curse, and trouble it.

"But all the silver and gold, and vessels of bronze and iron, are consecrated to the Lord; they shall come into the treasury of the Lord."

So the people shouted when the priests blew the trumpets. And it happened when the people heard the sound of the trumpet, and the people shouted with a great shout, that the wall fell down flat. Then the people went up into the city, every man straight before him, and they took the city.

Joshua 6:1-20 NKJV

And if it seem evil unto you to serve the Lord, choose you this day whom ye will serve; whether the gods which your fathers served that were on the other side of the flood, or the gods of the Amorites, in whose land ye dwell. but *as for me and my house, we will serve the Lord.*

Joshua 24:15

Then said David to the Philistine, Thou comest to me with a sword, and with a spear, and with a shield: but I come to thee in the name of the Lord of hosts, the God of the armies of Israel, whom thou hast defied.

This day will the Lord deliver thee into mine hand; and I will smite thee, and take thine head from thee; and I will give the carcases of the host of the Philistines this day unto the fowls of the air, and to the wild beasts of the earth; that all the earth may know that there is a God in Israel.

And all this assembly shall know that the Lord saveth not with sword and spear: for the battle is the Lord's, and he will give you into our hands.

And it came to pass, when the Philistine arose, and came and drew nigh to meet David, that David hasted, and ran toward the army to meet the Philistine.

And David put his hand in his bag, and took thence a stone, and slang it, and smote the Philistine in his forehead, that the stone sunk into his forehead; and he fell upon his face to the earth.

So David prevailed over the Philistine with a sling and with a stone, and smote the Philistine, and slew him; and there was no sword in the hand of David.

Therefore David ran, and stood upon the Philistine, and took his sword, and drew it out of the sheath thereof, and slew him, and cut off his head therewith. And when the Philistines saw their champion was dead, they fled.

1 Samuel 17:45-51

One day Elisha went to Shunem. And a well-to-do woman was there, who urged him to stay for a meal. So whenever he came by, he stopped there to eat. She said to her husband, "I know that this man who often comes our way is a holy man of God. Let's make a small room on the roof and put in it a bed and a table, a chair and a lamp for him. Then he can stay there whenever he comes to us."

One day when Elisha came, he went up to his room and lay down there. He said to his servant Gehazi, "Call the Shunammite." So he called her, and she stood before him. Elisha said to him, "Tell her, 'You have gone to all this trouble for us. Now what can be done for you? Can we speak on your behalf to the king or the commander of the army?'"

She replied, "I have a home among my own people."

"What can be done for her?" Elisha asked.

Gehazi said, "Well, she has no son and her husband is old."

Then Elisha said, "Call her." So he called her, and she stood in the doorway. "About this time next year," Elisha said, "you will hold a son in your arms."

"No, my lord," she objected. "Don't mislead your servant, O man of God!"

But the woman became pregnant, and the next year about that same time she gave birth to a son, just as Elisha had told her.

The child grew, and one day he went out to his father, who was with the reapers. "My head! My head!" he said to his father.

His father told a servant, "Carry him to his mother." After the servant had lifted him up and carried him to his mother, the boy sat on her lap until noon, and then he died. She went up and laid him on the bed of the man of God, then shut the door and went out.

She called her husband and said, "Please send me one of the servants and a donkey so I can go to the man of God quickly and return."

"Why go to him today?" he asked. "It's not the New Moon or the Sabbath."

"It's all right," she said.

She saddled the donkey and said to her servant, "Lead on; don't slow down for me unless I tell you." So she set out and came to the man of God at Mount Carmel.

When he saw her in the distance, the man of God said to his servant Gehazi, "Look! There's the Shunammite! Run to meet her and ask her, 'Are you all right? Is your husband all right? Is your child all right?'"

"Everything is all right," she said.

When she reached the man of God at the mountain, she took hold of his feet. Gehazi came over to push her away, but the man of God said, "Leave her alone! She is in bitter distress, but the Lord has hidden it from me and has not told me why."

"Did I ask you for a son, my lord?" she said. "Didn't I tell you, 'Don't raise my hopes'?"

Elisha said to Gehazi, "Tuck your cloak into your belt, take my staff in your hand and run. If you meet anyone, do not greet him, and if anyone greets you, do not answer. Lay my staff on the boy's face."

But the child's mother said, *"As surely as the Lord lives and as you live, I will not leave you."* So he got up and followed her.

Gehazi went on ahead and laid the staff on the boy's face, but there was no sound or response. So Gehazi went back to meet Elisha and told him, "The boy has not awakened."

When Elisha reached the house, there was the boy lying dead on his couch. He went in, shut the door on the two of them and prayed to the Lord. Then he got on the bed and lay upon the boy, mouth to mouth, eyes to eyes, hands to hands. As he stretched himself out upon him, the boy's body grew warm. Elisha turned away and walked back and forth in the room and then got on the bed and stretched out upon him once more. The boy sneezed seven times and opened his eyes.

Elisha summoned Gehazi and said, "Call the Shunammite." And he did. When she came, he said, "Take your son." She came in, fell at his feet and bowed to the ground. Then she took her son and went out.

2 Kings 4:8-37 NIV

I have set the Lord always before me: because he is at my right hand, I shall not be moved.

Psalm 16:8

For by You I can run through a troop, and by my God I can leap over a wall.

Psalm 18:29 AMP

Oh, love the Lord, all you His saints! For the Lord preserves the faithful, and fully repays the proud person.

Psalm 31:23 NIV

Commit thy way unto the Lord; trust also in him; and he shall bring it to pass.

Psalm 37:5

I waited patiently for the Lord; and he inclined unto me, and heard my cry.

Psalm 40:1

Nevertheless My lovingkindness I will not utterly take from him, nor allow My faithfulness to fail.

My covenant I will not break, nor alter the word that has gone out of My lips.

Psalm 89:33,34 NKJV

I will say of the Lord, He is my refuge and my fortress: my God; in him will I trust.

Psalm 91:2

For ever, O Lord, thy word is settled in heaven.

Thy faithfulness is unto all generations.

Psalm 119:89,90a

I wait for the Lord, my soul does wait, and in His word do I hope.

Psalm 130:5 NASB

Trust in the Lord with all thine heart; and lean not unto thine own understanding.

In all thy ways acknowledge him, and he shall direct thy paths.

Proverbs 3:5,6

Lean on, trust in, and be confident in the Lord with all your heart and mind and do not rely on your own insight or understanding.

In all your ways know, recognize, and acknowledge Him, and He will direct and make straight and plain your paths.

Proverbs 3:5,6 AMP

When thou liest down, thou shalt not be afraid: yea, thou shalt lie down, and thy sleep shall be sweet.

Be not afraid of sudden fear, neither of the desolation of the wicked, when it cometh.

For the Lord shall be thy confidence, and shall keep thy foot from being taken.

Proverbs 3:24-26

When you lie down, you will not be afraid; when you lie down, your sleep will be sweet.

Have no fear of sudden disaster or of the ruin that overtakes the wicked,

For the Lord will be your confidence and will keep your foot from being snared.

Proverbs 3:24-26 NIV

A faithful man shall abound with blessings.

Proverbs 28:20a

If you do not stand firm in your faith, you will not stand at all.

Isaiah 7:9b NIV

If you will not believe, you surely shall not last.

Isaiah 7:9b NASB

Thou wilt keep him in perfect peace, whose mind is stayed on thee: because he trusteth in thee.

Trust ye in the Lord for ever: for in the Lord JEHOVAH is everlasting strength.

Isaiah 26:3,4

Thou dost protect and prosper steadfast souls, for they rely on thee.

Always rely on the Eternal, for the Eternal's strength endures.

Isaiah 26:3,4
Moffatt's Translation

The grass withers and the flowers fall, but the word of our God stands forever.

Isaiah 40:8 NIV

But he was pierced for our transgressions, he was crushed for our iniquities; the punishment that brought us peace was upon him, and by his wounds we are healed.

Isaiah 53:5 NIV

So shall my word be that goeth forth out of my mouth: it shall not return unto me void, but it shall accomplish that which I please, and it shall prosper in the thing whereto I sent it.

For ye shall go out with joy, and be led forth with peace: the mountains and the hills shall break forth before you into singing, and all the trees of the field shall clap their hands.

Isaiah 55:11,12

For I am watching over My word to perform it.

Jeremiah 1:12b NASB

I am alert and active, watching over My word to perform it.

Jeremiah 1:12b AMP

Because of the Lord's great love we are not consumed, for his compassions never fail.

They are new every morning, great is your faithfulness.

Lamentations 3:22,23 NIV

For I am the Lord: I will speak, and the word that I shall speak shall come to pass;

Ezekiel 12:25a

Shadrach, Meshach and Abednego replied to the king, "O Nebuchadnezzar, we do not need to defend ourselves before you in this matter. If we are thrown into the blazing furnace, the God we serve is able to save us from it, and he will rescue us from your hand, O king. But even if he does not, we want you to know, O king, that we will not serve your gods or worship the image of gold you have set up."

Daniel 3:16-18 NIV

But the just shall live by his faith.

Habakkuk 2:4b

The righteous man trusts in me, and lives!

Habakkuk 2:4b TLB

New Testament

When praying, do not repeat the same words over and over again, as is done by the Gentiles, who think that by using many words they will obtain a hearing.

Do not imitate them; for God, your Father, knows what you need before you ask him.

Matthew 6:7,8

Therefore I say to you, do not worry about your life, what you will eat or what you will drink; nor about your body, what you will put on. Is not life more than food and the body more than clothing?

Look at the birds of the air, for they neither sow nor reap nor gather into barns; yet your heavenly Father feeds them. Are you not of more value than they?

Which of you by worrying can add one cubit to his stature?

So why do you worry about clothing? Consider the lilies of the field, how they grow: they neither toil nor spin;

And yet I say to you that even Solomon in all his glory was not arrayed like one of these.

Now if God so clothes the grass of the field, which today is, and tomorrow is thrown into the oven, will He not much more clothe you, O you of little faith?

Therefore do not worry, saying, "What shall we eat?" or "What shall we drink?" or "What shall we wear?"

For after all these things the Gentiles seek. For your heavenly Father knows that you need all these things.

But seek first the kingdom of God and His righteousness, and all these things shall be added to you.

Therefore do not worry about tomorrow, for tomorrow will worry about its own things. Sufficient for the day is its own trouble.

Matthew 6:25-34 NKJV

Keep on asking and it will be given you; keep on seeking and you will find; keep on knocking [reverently] and [the door] will be opened to you.

For everyone who keeps on asking receives; and he who keeps on seeking finds; and to him who keeps on knocking, [the door] will be opened.

Matthew 7:7,8 AMP

So everyone who hears these words of Mine and acts upon them [obeying them] will be like a sensible (prudent, practical, wise) man who built his house upon the rock.

And the rain fell and the floods came and the winds blew and beat against that house; yet it did not fall, because it had been founded on the rock.

And everyone who hears these words of Mine and does not do them will be like a stupid (foolish) man who built his house upon the sand.

And the rain fell and the floods came and the winds blew and beat against that house, and it fell—and great and complete was the fall of it.

Matthew 7:24-27 AMP

When Jesus had entered Capernaum, a centurion came to him, asking for help. "Lord," he said, "my servant lies at home paralyzed and in terrible suffering."

Jesus said to him, "I will go and heal him."

The centurion replied, "Lord, I do not deserve to have you come under my roof. But just say the word, and my servant will be healed. For I myself am a man under authority, with soldiers under me. I tell this one, 'Go,' and he goes; and that one, 'Come,' and he comes. I say to my servant, 'Do this,' and he does it."

When Jesus heard this, he was astonished and said to those following him, "I tell you the truth, I have not found anyone in Israel with such *great faith*. I say to you that many will come from the east and the west, and will take their places at the feast with Abraham, Isaac and Jacob in the kingdom of heaven. But the subjects of the kingdom will be thrown outside, into the darkness, where there will be weeping and gnashing of teeth."

Then Jesus said to the centurion, "Go! It will be done just as you believed it would." And his servant was healed at that very hour.

Matthew 8:5-13 NIV

And when he was entered into a ship, his disciples followed him. And, behold, there arose a great tempest in the sea, insomuch that the ship was covered with the waves: but he was asleep.

And his disciples came to him, and awoke him, saying, Lord, save us: we perish.

And he saith unto them, Why are ye fearful, O ye of little faith? Then he arose, and rebuked the winds and the sea; and there was a great calm.

But the men marvelled, saying, What manner of man is this, that even the winds and the sea obey him!

Matthew 8:23-27

And behold, they were bringing to Him a paralytic, lying on a bed; and Jesus seeing their faith said to the paralytic, "Take courage, My son, your sins are forgiven."

And behold, some of the scribes said to themselves, "This fellow blasphemes."

And Jesus knowing their thoughts said, "Why are you thinking evil in your hearts?

"For which is easier, to say, 'Your sins are forgiven,' or to say, 'Rise, and walk'?

"But in order that you may know that the Son of Man has authority on earth to forgive sins"—then He said to the paralytic, "Rise, take up your bed, and go home."

And he rose, and went to his home.

Matthew 9:2-7 NASB

While He spoke these things to them, behold, a ruler came and worshiped Him, saying, "My daughter has just died, but come and lay Your hand on her and she will live."

So Jesus arose and followed him, and so did His disciples.

And suddenly, a woman who had a flow of blood for twelve years came from behind and touched the hem of His garment.

For she said to herself, "If only I may touch His garment, I shall be made well."

But Jesus turned around, and when He saw her He said, "Be of good cheer, daughter; *your faith has made you well.*" And the women was made well from that hour.

When Jesus came into the ruler's house, and saw the flute players and the noisy crowd wailing,

He said to them, "Make room, for the girl is not dead, but sleeping." And they ridiculed Him.

But when the crowd was put outside, He went in and took her by the hand, and the girl arose.

Matthew 9:18-25 NKJV

And when Jesus departed thence, two blind men followed him, crying, and saying, Thou Son of David, have mercy on us.

And when he was come into the house, the blind men came to him: and Jesus saith unto them, *Believe ye that I am able to do this? They said unto him, Yea, Lord.*

Then touched he their eyes, saying, *According to your faith be it unto you.*

And their eyes were opened; and Jesus straitly charged them, saying, See that no man know it.

But they, when they were departed, spread abroad his fame in all that country.

Matthew 9:27-31

After dismissing the crowds, he went up the hill by himself to pray; and, when evening fell, he was there alone.

The boat was by this time some miles from shore, labouring in the waves, for the wind was against her.

Three hours after midnight, however, Jesus came towards the disciples, walking on the water. But, when they saw him walking on the water, they were terrified.

"It is a ghost," they exclaimed, and cried out for fear. But Jesus at once spoke to them.

"Courage!" he said, "It is I; do not be afraid!"

"Master," Peter exclaimed, "if it is you, tell me to come to you on the water."

And Jesus said: "Come." So Peter got down from the boat, and walked on the water, and went towards Jesus; but, when he felt the wind, he was frightened, and, beginning to sink, cried out: "Master! Save me!" Instantly Jesus stretched out his hand, and caught hold of him.

"O man of little faith!" he said, "Why did you falter?" When they had got into the boat, the wind dropped. But the men in the boat threw themselves on their faces before him, and said: "You are indeed God's Son."

Matthew 14:23-33
The Twentieth Century
New Testament

And when they came to the multitude, a man came up to Him, falling on his knees before Him, and saying,

"Lord, have mercy on my son, for he is an epileptic, and is very ill; for he often falls into the fire, and often into the water.

"And I brought him to Your disciples, and they could not cure him."

And Jesus answered and said, "O unbelieving and perverted generation, how long shall I be with you? How long shall I put up with you? Bring him here to Me."

And Jesus rebuked him, and the demon came out of him, and the boy was cured at once.

Then the disciples came to Jesus privately and said, "Why could we not cast it out?"

And He said to them, "Because of the littleness of your faith; for truly I say to you, if you have faith as a mustard seed, you shall say to this mountain, 'Move from here to there,' and it shall move; and nothing shall be impossible to you."

Matthew 17:14-20 NASB

With God all things are possible.

Matthew 19:26b

Jesus looked at them and said, "This is impossible for men, but anything is possible for God."

Matthew 19:26
Moffatt's Translation

And Jesus answered them, Truly I say to you, if you have faith (a firm relying trust) and do not doubt, you will not only do what has been done to the fig tree, but even if you say to this mountain, Be taken up and cast into the sea, it will be done.

And whatever you ask for in prayer, *having faith and [really] believing, you will receive.*

Matthew 21:21,22 AMP

Heaven and earth will pass away, but my words never!

Matthew 24:35
Moffatt's Translation

And he said unto them, Take heed what ye hear: with what measure ye mete, it shall be measured to you: and unto you that hear shall more be given.

For he that hath, to him shall be given: and he that hath not, from him shall be taken even that which he hath.

And he said, So is the kingdom of God, as if a man should cast seed into the ground;

And should sleep, and rise night and day, and the seed should spring and grow up, he knoweth not how.

For the earth bringeth forth fruit of herself, first the blade, then the ear, after that the full corn in the ear.

But when the fruit is brought forth, immediately he putteth in the sickle, because the harvest is come.

And he said, Whereunto shall we liken the kingdom of God? Or with what comparison shall we compare it?

It is like a grain of mustard seed, which, when it is sown in the earth, is less than all the seeds that be in the earth:

But when it is sown, it groweth up, and becometh greater than all herbs, and shooteth out great branches; so that the fowls of the air may lodge under the shadow of it.

Mark 4:24-32

With men, impossible, but not in the presence of God, for all things are possible in the presence of God.

Mark 10:27
The Wuest New Testament

"What do you want me to do for you?" Jesus asked him.

The blind man said, "Rabbi, I want to see."

"Go," said Jesus, "your faith has healed you." Immediately he received his sight and followed Jesus along the road.

Mark 10:51,52 NIV

"Have faith in God," Jesus answered. "I tell you the truth, if anyone says to this mountain, 'Go, throw yourself into the sea,' and does not doubt in his heart but believes that what he says will happen, it will be done for him. Therefore I tell you, whatever you ask for in prayer, believe that you have received it, and it will be yours. And when you stand praying, if you hold anything against anyone, forgive him, so that your Father in heaven may forgive you your sins."

Mark 11:22-26 NIV

For no promise of God can fail to be fulfilled.

Luke 1:37
J.B. Phillips Translation

No word from God shall be without power.

Luke 1:37
The Worrell New Testament

Blessed is she who has believed that what the Lord has said to her will be accomplished!

Luke 1:45 NIV

And he said to her, "Your sins are forgiven." His fellow guests began to say to themselves, "Who is this, to forgive even sins?" But he said to the woman, "Your faith has saved you; go in peace."

Luke 7:48-50
Moffatt's Translation

His apostles asked him what the story meant.

36

He replied, "God has granted you to know the meaning of these parables, for they tell a great deal about the Kingdom of God. But these crowds hear the words and do not understand, just as the ancient prophets predicted.

"This is the meaning: The seed is God's message to men. The hard path where some seed fell represents the hard hearts of those who hear the words of God, but then the devil comes and steals the words away and prevents people from believing and being saved.

"The stony ground represents those who enjoy listening to sermons, but somehow the message never really gets through to them and doesn't take root and grow. They know the message is true, and sort of believe for awhile; but when the hot winds of persecution blow, they lose interest.

"The seed among the thorns represents those who listen and believe God's words but whose faith afterwards is choked out by worry and riches and the responsibilities and pleasures of life. And so they are never able to help anyone else to believe the Good News.

"But the good soil represents honest, good-hearted people. They listen to God's words and cling to them and steadily spread them to others who also soon believe."

Luke 8:9-15 TLB

And I say unto you, Ask, and it shall be given you; seek, and ye shall find; knock, and it shall be opened unto you.

For every one that asketh receiveth; and he that seeketh findeth; and to him that knocketh it shall be opened.

Luke 11:9,10

He that is faithful in that which is least is faithful also in much.

Luke 16:10a

And the apostles said to the Lord, "Increase our faith!"

And the Lord said, "If you had faith like a mustard seed, you would say to this mulberry tree, 'Be uprooted and be planted in the sea'; and it would obey you."

Luke 17:5,6 NASB

And it came to pass that as He was proceeding on His way to Jerusalem, He also himself was going through the midst of Samaria and Galilee. And as He was entering a certain village there met Him ten lepers, men, who stood at a distance, and they themselves raised their voice, saying, Jesus, Master, you who have power and authority, be sympathetic with our affliction and do something to help us.

And having seen them He said to them, Having gone on your way, show yourselves as proof to the priests. And it came to pass that while they were going, they were cleansed.

And one of them, having seen that he was healed, returned with a loud voice, glorifying God, and fell on his face at His feet, expressing his gratitude to Him. And he himself was a Samaritan.

And answering, Jesus said, Were not the ten cleansed? But the nine, where are they? Were they not found returning to give glory to God except this foreigner? And He said to him, Having arisen, be going on your way. *Your faith has restored your body to soundness of health.*

Luke 17:11-19
The Wuest New Testament

The things which are impossible with men are possible with God.

Luke 18:27

Saying, What wilt thou that I shall do unto thee? And he said, Lord, that I may receive my sight.

And Jesus said unto him, Receive thy sight: thy faith hath saved thee.

And immediately he received his sight, and followed him, glorifying God: and all the people, when they saw it, gave praise unto God.

Luke 18:41-43

"Simon, Simon, behold, Satan asked for you, to sift you as the wheat;

"But I prayed for you, that your faith fail not; and, when once you have turned again, establish your brethren."

Luke 22:31,32
The Worrell New Testament

Simon! Simon! Listen. Satan demanded leave to sift you all like wheat, but I prayed for you, Simon, that your faith should not fail. And you, when you have returned to me, are to strengthen your brothers.

Luke 22:31,32
The Twentieth Century
New Testament

But as many as received him, to them gave he power to become the sons of God, even to them that believe on his name.

John 1:12

For God so loved the world, that he gave his only begotten Son, that whosoever believeth in him should not perish, but have everlasting life.

For God sent not his Son into the world to condemn the world; but that the world through him might be saved.

John 3:16,17

And a certain man was there, which had an infirmity thirty and eight years.

When Jesus saw him lie, and knew that he had been now a long time in that case, he saith unto him, Wilt thou be made whole?

The impotent man answered him, Sir, I have no man, when the water is troubled, to put me into the pool: but while I am coming, another steppeth down before me.

Jesus saith unto him, Rise, take up thy bed, and walk.

And immediately the man was made whole, and took up his bed, and walked: and on the same day was the sabbath.

John 5:5-9

This is the work of God, that ye believe on him whom he hath sent.

John 6:29b

He that believeth on me, as the scripture hath said, out of his belly shall flow rivers of living water.

John 7:38

"Do you believe in the Son of Man?"

"Tell me who he is, Sir," he replied, "so that I may believe in him."

"Not only have you seen him," said Jesus; "but it is he who is now speaking to you."

"Then, Sir, I do believe," said the man, bowing to the ground before him.

John 9:35b-38
The Twentieth Century
New Testament

If I do not the works of my Father, believe me not.

But if I do, though ye believe not me, believe the works: that ye may know, and believe, that the Father is in me, and I in him.

John 10:37,38

Jesus said, "Take away the stone [from Lazarus' grave]." Martha, the sister of him who was dead, said to Him, "Lord, by this time there is a stench, for he has been dead four days."

Jesus said to her, "Did I not say to you that if you would believe you would see the glory of God?"

Then they took away the stone from the place where the dead man was lying. And Jesus lifted up His eyes and said, "Father, I thank You that You have heard Me.

"And I know that You always hear Me, but because of the people who are standing by I said this, that they may believe that You sent Me."

Now when He had said these things, He cried with a loud voice, "Lazarus, come forth!"

And he who had died came out bound hand and foot with graveclothes, and his face was wrapped with a cloth. Jesus said to them, "Loose him, and let him go."

Then many of the Jews who had come to Mary, and had seen the things Jesus did, believed in Him.

John 11:39-45 NKJV

Don't you believe that I am in the Father, and that the Father is in me? The words I say to you are not just my own. Rather, it is the Father, living in me, who is doing his work. Believe me when I say that I am in the Father and the Father is in me; or at least believe on the evidence of the miracles themselves.

I tell you the truth, anyone who has faith in me will do what I have been doing. He will do even greater things than these, because I am going to the Father.

And I will do whatever you ask in my name, so that the Son may bring glory to the Father. You may ask me for anything in my name, and I will do it.

John 14:10-14 NIV

Now Thomas, called the Twin, one of the twelve, was not with them when Jesus came.

The other disciples therefore said to him, "We have seen the Lord." So he said to them, "Unless I see in His hands the print of the nails, and put my finger into the print of the nails, and put my hand into His side, I will not believe."

And after eight days His disciples were again inside, and Thomas with them. Jesus came, the doors being shut, and stood in the midst, and said, "Peace to you!"

Then He said to Thomas, "Reach your finger here, and look at My hands; and reach your hand here, and put it into My side. Do not be unbelieving, but believing."

And Thomas answered and said to Him, "My Lord and my God!"

Jesus said to him, "Thomas, because you have seen Me, you have believed. Blessed are those who have not seen and yet have believed."

John 20:24-30 NKJV

Now Peter and John were going up to the temple at the ninth hour, the hour of prayer.

And a certain man who had been lame from his mother's womb was being carried along, whom they used to set down every day at the gate of the temple which is called Beautiful, in order to beg alms of those who were entering the temple.

And when he saw Peter and John about to go into the temple, he began asking to receive alms.

And Peter, along with John, fixed his gaze upon him and said, "Look at us!"

And he began to give them his attention, expecting to receive something from them.

But Peter said, "I do not possess silver and gold, but what I do have I give to you: In the name of Jesus Christ the Nazarene—walk!"

And seizing him by the right hand, he raised him up; and immediately his feet and his ankles were strengthened.

And with a leap, he stood upright and began to walk; and he entered the temple with them, walking and leaping and praising God.

And on the basis of faith in His name, it is the name of Jesus which has strengthened this man whom you see and know; and the faith which comes through Him has given him this perfect health in the presence of you all.

Acts 3:1-8,16 NASB

Many of those who heard the word believed; and the number of the men came to be about five thousand.

Acts 4:4 NKJV

And Stephen, full of faith and power, did great wonders and miracles among the people.

Acts 6:8

Wherefore, sirs, be of good cheer: for I believe God, that it shall be even as it was told me.

Acts 27:25

Therefore, courage, my friends! For I believe God, that everything will happen exactly as I have been told.

Acts 27:25
The Twentieth Century
New Testament

So keep up your courage, men, for I have faith (complete confidence) in God that it will be exactly as it was told me.

Acts 27:25 AMP

First, I thank my God through Jesus Christ for you all, that your faith is spoken of throughout the whole world.

Romans 1:8

For I am not ashamed of the gospel of Christ: for it is the power of God unto salvation to every one that believeth; to the Jew first, and also to the Greek.

For therein is the righteousness of God revealed from faith to faith: as it is written, The just shall live by faith.

Romans 1:16,17

For what if some did not believe? shall their unbelief make the faith of God without effect?

God forbid: yea, let God be true, but every man a liar; as it is written, That thou mightest be justified in thy sayings, and mightest overcome when thou art judged.

Romans 3:3,4

Therefore by the deeds of the law there shall no flesh be justified in his sight: for by the law is the knowledge of sin.

But now the righteousness of God without the law is manifested, being witnessed by the law and the prophets;

Even the righteousness of God which is by faith of Jesus Christ unto all and upon all them that believe: for there is no difference:

For all have sinned, and come short of the glory of God;

Being justified freely by his grace through the redemption that is in Christ Jesus:

Whom God hath set forth to be a propitiation through faith in his blood, to declare his righteousness for the remission of sins that are past, through the forbearance of God;

To declare, I say, at this time his righteousness: that he might be just, and the justifier of him which believeth in Jesus.

Where is boasting then? It is excluded. By what law? Of works? Nay: but by the law of faith.

Therefore we conclude that a man is justified by faith without the deeds of the law.

Is he the God of the Jews only? Is he not also of the Gentiles? Yes, of the Gentiles also:

Seeing it is one God, which shall justify the circumcision by faith, and uncircumcision through faith.

Do we then make void the law through faith? God forbid: yea, we establish the law.

Romans 3:20-31

What then shall we say that Abraham, our fore-father, discovered in this matter? If, in fact, Abraham was justified by works, he had something to boast about—but not before God. What does the Scripture say? "Abraham believed God, and it was credited to him as righteousness."

Now when a man works, his wages are not credited to him as a gift, but as an obligation. However, to the man who does not work but trusts God who justifies the wicked, his faith is credited as righteousness.

Romans 4:1-5 NIV

We have been saying that Abraham's faith was credited to him as righteousness. Under what circumstances was it credited? Was it after he was circumcised, or before? It was not after, but before! And he received the sign of circumcision, a seal of the righteousness that he had by faith while he was still uncircumcised. So then, he is the father of all who believe but have not been circumcised, in order that righteousness might be credited to them. And he is also the father of the circumcised who not only are circumcised but who also walk in the footsteps of the faith that our father Abraham had before he was circumcised.

It was not through law that Abraham and his offspring received the promise that he would be heir of the world, but through the righteousness that comes by faith. For if those who live by law are heirs, faith has no value and the promise is worthless, because law brings wrath. And where there is no law there is no transgression.

Therefore, the promise comes by faith, so that it *may* be by grace and may be guaranteed to all Abraham's offspring not only to those who are of the law but also to those who are of the faith of Abraham. He is the father of us all. As it is written: "I have made you a father of many nations." He is our father in the sight of God, in whom he believed—the God who gives life to the dead and *calls things that are not as though they were.*

Against all hope, Abraham in hope believed and so became the father of many nations, just as it had been said to him, "So shall your offspring be." Without weakening in his faith, he faced the fact that his body was as good as dead—since he was about a hundred years old—and that Sarah's womb was also dead. Yet he did not waver through unbelief regarding the promise of God, but was strengthened in his faith and gave glory to God, being fully persuaded that God had power to do what he had promised. This is why "it was credited to him as righteousness." The words "it was credited to him" were written not for him alone, but also for us, to whom God will credit righteousness—for us who believe in him who raised Jesus our Lord from the dead. He was delivered over to death for our sins and was raised to life for our justification.

Romans 4:9b-25 NIV

Therefore being justified by faith, we have peace with God through our Lord Jesus Christ:

By whom also we have access by faith into this grace wherein we stand, and rejoice in hope of the glory of God.

Romans 5:1,2

So now, since we have been made right in God's sight by faith in his promises, we can have real peace with him because of what Jesus Christ our Lord has done for us.

For because of our faith, he has brought us into this place of highest privilege where we now stand, and we confidently and joyfully look forward to actually becoming all that God has had in mind for us to be.

Romans 5:1,2 TLB

There is, therefore, now no condemnation for those who are in union with Christ Jesus; for through your union with Christ Jesus, the Law of the life-giving Spirit has set you free from the Law of Sin and Death.

Romans 8:1
The Twentieth Century
New Testament

But if the Spirit of him that raised up Jesus from the dead dwell in you, he that raised up Christ from the dead shall also quicken your mortal bodies by his Spirit that dwelleth in you.

Romans 8:11

If God be for us, who can be against us?

Romans 8:31b

What shall we say then? That Gentiles, who did not pursue righteousness, attained righteousness, even the righteousness which is by faith;

But Israel, pursuing a law of righteousness, did not arrive at that law.

Why? Because they did not pursue it by faith, but as though it were by works. They stumbled over the stumbling stone,

Just as it is written, "Behold, I lay in Zion a stone of stumbling and a rock of offense, and he who believes in Him will not be disappointed."

Romans 9:30-33 NASB

But the righteousness of faith speaks in this way, "Do not say in your heart, 'Who will ascend into heaven?'" (that is, to bring Christ down from above). "Or, 'Who will descend into the abyss?'" (that is, to bring Christ up from the dead).

But what does it say? "The word is near you, in your mouth and in your heart" (that is, the word of faith which we preach):

That if you confess with your mouth the Lord Jesus and believe in your heart that God has raised Him from the dead, you will be saved.

For with the heart one believes unto righteousness, and with the mouth confession is made unto salvation.

For the Scripture says, "Whoever believes on Him will not be put to shame."

For there is no distinction between Jew and Greek, for the same Lord over all is rich to all who call upon Him.

For "whoever calls on the name of the Lord shall be saved."

How then shall they call on Him in whom they have not believed? And how shall they believe in Him of whom they have not heard? And how shall they hear without a preacher?

And how shall they preach unless they are sent? As it is written: "How beautiful are the feet of those who preach the gospel of peace, who bring glad tidings of good things!"

But they have not all obeyed the gospel. For Isaiah says, "Lord, who has believed our report?"

So then faith comes by hearing, and hearing by the word of God.

Romans 10:6-17 NIV

If the first handful of dough is consecrated, so is the rest of the lump; if the root is consecrated, so are the branches.

Supposing some of the branches have been broken off, while you have been grafted in, like a shoot of wild olive to share the rich growth of the olive-stem, do not pride yourself at the expense of these branches. Remember, in your pride, the stem supports you, not you the stem.

You will say, "But branches were broken off, to let me be grafted in!" Granted. They were broken off — for their lack of faith. And you owe your position to your faith. You should feel awed instead of being uplifted. For if God did not spare the natural branches, he will not spare you either.

Consider both the kindness and the severity of God; those who fall come under his severity, but you come under the divine kindness, provided you adhere to that kindness. Otherwise, you will be cut away too. And even the others will be grafted in, if they do not adhere to their unbelief, God can graft them in again.

Romans 11:16-23
Moffatt's Translation

God hath dealt to every man the measure of faith.

Romans 12:3b

The faith which you have, have as your own conviction before God. Happy is he who does not condemn himself in what he approves.

But he who doubts is condemned if he eats, because his eating is not from faith; and whatever is not from faith is sin.

Romans 14:22,23 NASB

You may know that there is nothing wrong with what you do, even from God's point of view, but keep it to yourself; don't flaunt your faith in front of others who might be hurt by it. In this situation, happy is the man who does not sin by doing what he knows is right.

But anyone who believes that something he wants to do is wrong shouldn't do it. He sins if he does, for he thinks it is wrong, and so for him it is wrong. Anything that is done apart from what he feels is right is sin.

Romans 14:22,23 TLB

Now the God of hope fill you with all joy and peace in believing, that ye may abound in hope, through the power of the Holy Ghost.

Romans 15:13

May God, who inspires our hope, grant you perfect happiness and *peace* in your faith, till you are filled with this hope by the power of the Holy Spirit.

Romans 15:13
The Twentieth Century
New Testament

God will surely do this for you, for he always does just what he says, and he is the one who invited you into this wonderful friendship with his Son, even Christ our Lord.

1 Corinthians 1:9 TLB

For God in his wisdom saw to it that the world would never find God through human brilliance, and then he stepped in and saved all those who believed his message, which the world calls foolish and silly.

It seems foolish to the Jews because they want a sign from heaven as proof that what is preached is true; and it is foolish to the Gentiles because they believe only what agrees with their philosophy and seems wise to them.

So when we preach about Christ dying to save them, the Jews are offended and the Gentiles say it's all nonsense.

But God has opened the eyes of those called to salvation, both Jews and Gentiles, to see that Christ is the mighty power of God to save them; Christ himself is the center of God's wise plan for their salvation.

This so-called "foolish" plan of God is far wiser than the wisest plan of the wisest man, and God in his weakness—Christ dying on the cross—is far stronger than any man.

Notice among yourselves, dear brothers, that few of you who follow Christ have big names or power or wealth.

Instead, God has deliberately chosen to use ideas the world considers foolish and of little worth in order to shame those people considered by the world as wise and great.

He has chosen a plan despised by the world, counted as nothing at all, and used it to bring down to nothing those the world considers great,

So that no one anywhere can ever brag in the presence of God.

For it is from God alone that you have your life through Christ Jesus. He showed us God's plan of salvation; he was the one who made us acceptable to God; he made us pure and holy and gave himself to purchase our salvation.

As it says in the Scriptures, "If anyone is going to boast, let him boast only of what the Lord has done."

1 Corinthians 1:21-31 TLB

And my speech and my preaching was not with enticing words of man's wisdom, but in demonstration of the Spirit and of power:

That your faith should not stand in the wisdom of men, but in the power of God.

1 Corinthians 2:4,5

And my message and my preaching were not couched in specious words of philosophy but were dependent for their efficacy upon a demonstration of the Spirit and of power, in order that your faith should not be resting in human philosophy but in God's power.

1 Corinthians 2:4,5
The Wuest New Testament

But the manifestation of the Spirit is given to every man to profit withal. For to one is given by the Spirit the word of wisdom; to another the word of knowledge by the same Spirit;

To another *faith by the same Spirit;* to another the gifts of healing by the same Spirit;

To another the working of miracles; to another prophecy; to another discerning of spirits; to another divers kinds of tongues; to another the interpretation of tongues:

But all these worketh that one and the self-same Spirit, dividing to every man severally as he will.

1 Corinthians 12:7-11

And though I have the gift of prophecy, and understand all mysteries, and all knowledge; and though I have all faith, so that I could remove mountains, and have not charity, I am nothing.

1 Corinthians 13:2

Be on your guard; stand firm in the faith; be men of courage; be strong. Do everything in love.

1 Corinthians 16:13,14 NIV

For no matter how many promises God has made, they are "Yes" in Christ. And so through him the "Amen" is spoken by us to the glory of God.

2 Corinthians 1:20 NIV

For in him [Jesus Christ] is the "yes" that affirms all the promises of God. Hence it is through him that we affirm our "amen" in worship, to the glory of God.

2 Corinthians 1:20
Moffatt's Translation

Not that we lord it over your faith, but we work with you for your joy, because it is by faith you stand firm.

2 Corinthians 1:24 NIV

And since we have the same spirit of faith, according to what is written, "I believed and therefore I spoke," we also believe and therefore speak.

2 Corinthians 4:13 NKJV

But since our spirit of faith is the same, therefore—as it is written I believed and so I spoke—I too believe and so I speak.

2 Corinthians 4:13
Moffatt's Translation

Therefore, as I said, we do not lose heart. No, even though outwardly we are wasting away, yet inwardly we are being renewed day by day.

The light burden of our momentary trouble is preparing for us, in measure transcending thought, a weight of imperishable glory;

We, all the while, gazing not on what is seen, but on what is unseen; for what is seen is transient, but what is unseen is imperishable.

2 Corinthians 4:16-18
The Twentieth Century
New Testament

For we walk by faith, not by sight.

2 Corinthians 5:7

And, remembering how you excel in every-thing—in faith, in teaching, in knowledge, in unfailing earnestness, and in the affection that we have awakened in you—I ask you to excel also in this expression of your love.

2 Corinthians 8:7
The Twentieth Century
New Testament

The truth is that, although we lead normal human lives, the battle we are fighting is on the spiritual level.

The very weapons we use are not human but powerful in God's warfare for the destruction of the enemy's strongholds.

Our battle is to break down every deceptive argument and every imposing defence that men erect against the true knowledge of God. We fight to capture every thought until it acknowledges the authority of Christ.

2 Corinthians 10:3-5
J.B. Phillips Translation

Examine yourselves as to whether you are in the faith. Test yourselves. Do you not know yourselves, that Jesus Christ is in you?—unless indeed you are disqualified.

But I trust that you will know that we are not disqualified.

2 Corinthians 13:5,6 NKJV

Knowing that a man is not justified by the works of the law, but by the faith of Jesus Christ, even we have believed in Jesus Christ, that we

65

might be justified by the faith of Christ, and not by the works of the law: for by the works of the law shall no flesh be justified.

Galatians 2:16

I am crucified with Christ nevertheless I live; yet not I, but Christ liveth in me: and the life which I now live in the flesh I live by the faith of the Son of God, who loved me, and gave himself for me.

Galatians 2:20

You foolish Galatians! Who has bewitched you? Before your very eyes Jesus Christ was clearly portrayed as crucified. I would like to learn just one thing from you: Did you receive the Spirit by observing the law, or by believing what you heard? Are you so foolish? After beginning with the Spirit, are you now trying to attain your goal by human effort? Have you suffered so much for nothing—if it really was for nothing? Does God give you his Spirit and work miracles among you because you observe the law, or because you believe what you heard?

Consider Abraham: "He believed God, and it was credited to him as righteousness." Understand, then, that those who believe are children of Abraham. The Scripture foresaw that God would justify the Gentiles by faith, and announced the gospel in advance to Abraham: "All nations will be blessed through you." So those who have faith are blessed along with Abraham, the man of faith.

All who rely on observing the law are under a curse, for it is written: "Cursed is everyone who does not continue to do everything written in the Book of the Law." Clearly no one is justified before God by the law, because, "The righteous will live by faith." The law is not based on faith; on the contrary, "The man who does these things will live by them." Christ redeemed us from the curse of the law by becoming a curse for us, for it is written: "Cursed is everyone who is hung on a tree." He redeemed us in order that the blessing given to Abraham might come to the Gentiles through Christ Jesus, so that by faith we might receive the promise of the Spirit.

Galatians 3:1-14 NIV

But the scripture hath concluded all under sin, that the promise by faith of Jesus Christ might be given to them that believe.

But before faith came, we were kept under the law, shut up unto the faith which should afterwards be revealed.

Wherefore the law was our schoolmaster to bring us unto Christ, that we might be justified by faith.

But after that faith is come, we are no longer under a schoolmaster.

For ye are all the children of God by faith in Christ Jesus.

Galatians 3:22-26

The only thing that counts is *faith expressing itself through love.*

Galatians 5:6 NIV

And what is the exceeding greatness of his power to usward who believe, according to the working of his mighty power,

Which he wrought in Christ, when he raised him from the dead, and set him at his own right hand in the heavenly places,

Far above all principality, and power, and might, and dominion, and every name that is named, not only in this world, but also in that which is to come:

And hath put all things under his feet, and gave him to be the head over all things to the church,

Which is his body, the fulness of him that filleth all in all.

Ephesians 1:19-23

For it is by free grace (God's unmerited favor) that you are saved (delivered from judgment and made partakers of Christ's salvation) through [your] faith. And this [salvation] is not of yourselves [of your own doing, it came not through your own striving], but it is the gift of God.

Ephesians 2:8 AMP

In whom [in Christ] we have boldness and access with confidence by the faith of him.

Ephesians 3:12

It is in this same Jesus, because we have faith in him, that we dare, even with confidence, to approach God.

Ephesians 3:12
J.B. Phillips Translation

Be strong in the Lord [be empowered through your union with Him]; draw your strength from Him [that strength which His boundless might provides].

Put on God's whole armor [the armor of a heavy-armed soldier which God supplies], that you may be able successfully to stand up against [all] the strategies and the deceits of the devil.

For we are not wrestling with flesh and blood [contending only with physical opponents], but against the despotisms, against the powers, against [the master spirits who are] the world rulers of this present darkness, in the heavenly (supernatural) sphere.

Therefore put on God's complete armor, that you may be able to resist and stand your ground on the evil day [of danger], and, having done all [the crisis demands], to stand [firmly in your place].

Stand therefore [hold your ground], having tightened the belt of truth around your loins and having put on the breastplate of integrity and of moral rectitude and right standing with God,

And having shod your feet in preparation [to face the enemy with the firmfooted stability, the promptness, and the readiness produced by the good news] of the Gospel of peace.

Lift up over all the [covering] shield of saving faith, upon which you can quench all the flaming missiles of the wicked [one].

And take the helmet of salvation and the sword that the Spirit wields, which is the Word of God.

Pray at all times (on every occasion, in every season) in the Spirit, with all [manner of] prayer and entreaty. To that end keep alert and watch with strong purpose and perseverance, interceding in behalf of all the saints (God's consecrated people).

Ephesians 6:10-18 AMP

Yea doubtless, and I count all things but loss for the excellency of the knowledge of Christ Jesus my Lord: for whom I have suffered the loss of all things, and do count them but dung, that I may win Christ,

And be found in him, not having mine own righteousness, which is of the law, but that which is through the faith of Christ, the righteousness which is of God by faith:

That I may know him, and the power of his resurrection, and the fellowship of his sufferings, being made conformable unto his death.

Philippians 3:8-10

And you, who once were alienated and enemies in your mind by wicked works, yet now He has reconciled

In the body of His flesh through death, to present you holy, and blameless, and above reproach in His sight.

Colossians 1:21-23 NKJV

But as for us who are of the day, let us be mentally and spiritually well-balanced and self-controlled, having clothed ourselves with a breastplate of faith and love, and for a helmet, a hope of salvation.

1 Thessalonians 5:8
The Wuest New Testament

We ought always to thank God for you, brothers, and rightly so, because your faith is growing more and more, and the love every one of you has for each other is increasing. Therefore, among God's churches we boast about your perseverance and faith in all the persecutions and trials you are enduring.

2 Thessalonians 1:3,4 NIV

With this in mind, we constantly pray for you, that our God may count you worthy of his calling, and that by his power he may fulfill every good purpose of yours and every act prompted by your faith. We pray this so that the name of our Lord Jesus may be glorified in you, and you in him, according to the grace of our God and the Lord Jesus Christ.

2 Thessalonians 1:11,12 NIV

And the grace of our Lord was exceedingly abundant, with faith and love which are in Christ Jesus.

1 Timothy 1:14 NKJV

This, then, is the charge that I lay upon you, Timothy, my Child, in accordance with what was predicted of you — Fight the good fight in the spirit of those predictions, with faith, and with a clear conscience; and it is because they have thrust this aside, that, as regards the Faith, some have wrecked their lives.

1 Timothy 1:18,19
The Twentieth Century
New Testament

Deacons in turn are to be serious men; they are not to be tale-bearers nor addicted to drink or pilfering, they must maintain the divine truth of the faith with a pure conscience.

1 Timothy 3:8,9
Moffatt's Translation

Don't let anyone look down on you because you are young, but set an example for the believers in speech, in life, in love, in faith and in purity.

Until I come, devote yourself to the public reading of Scripture, to preaching and to teaching.

Do not neglect your gift, which was given you through a prophetic message when the body of elders laid their hands on you.

Be diligent in these matters; give yourself wholly to them, so that everyone may see your progress.

Watch your life and doctrine closely. Persevere in them, because if you do, you will save both yourself and your hearers.

1 Timothy 4:12-16 NIV

But thou, O man of God, flee these things; and follow after righteousness, godliness, faith, love, patience, meekness.

Fight the good fight of faith, lay hold on eternal life, whereunto thou art also called, and hast professed a good profession before many witnesses.

1 Timothy 6:11,12

For this reason I also suffer these things, but I am not ashamed; for I know whom I have believed and I am convinced that He is able to guard what I have entrusted to Him until that day.

Retain the standard of sound words which you have heard from me, in the faith and love which are in Christ Jesus.

Guard, through the Holy Spirit who dwells in us, the treasure which has been entrusted to you.

2 Timothy 1:12-14 NASB

Here is a trustworthy saying: If we died with him, we will also live with him;

If we endure, we will also reign with him. If we disown him, he will also disown us;

If we are faithless, he will remain faithful, for he cannot disown himself.

2 Timothy 2:11-13 NIV

Flee the evil desires of youth, and pursue righteousness, faith, love and peace, along with those who call on the Lord out of a pure heart.

2 Timothy 2:22 NIV

I have fought the good fight, I have finished the course, I have kept the faith.

2 Timothy 4:7 NASB

I have run the great Race; I have finished the Course; I have kept the Faith. And now the crown of righteousness awaits me, which the Lord, the just Judge, will give me on "That Day" — and not only to me, but to all who have loved his Appearing.

2 Timothy 4:7,8
The Twentieth Century
New Testament

I thank my God, making mention of thee always in my prayers,

Hearing of thy love and faith, which thou hast toward the Lord Jesus, and toward all saints;

That the communication of thy faith may become effectual by the acknowledging of every good thing which is in you in Christ Jesus.

Philemon 4-6

Let us therefore fear, lest, a promise being left us of entering into his rest, any of you should seem to come short of it.

For unto us was the gospel preached, as well as unto them: but the word preached did not profit them, not being mixed with faith in them that heard it.

For we which have believed do enter into rest.

Hebrews 4:1-3a

For the word of God is living and active. Sharper than any double-edged sword, it penetrates even to dividing soul and spirit, joints and marrow; it judges the thoughts and attitudes of the heart. Nothing in all creation is hidden from God's sight.

Everything is uncovered and laid bare before the eyes of him to whom we must give account.

Therefore, since we have a great high priest who has gone through the heavens, Jesus the Son of God, let us hold firmly to the faith we profess. For we do not have a high priest who is unable to sympathize with our weaknesses, but we have one who has been tempted in every way, just as we are—yet was without sin. Let us then approach the throne of grace with confidence, so that we may receive mercy and find grace to help us in our time of need.

Hebrews 4:12-16 NIV

Therefore leaving the principles of the doctrine of Christ, let us go on unto perfection; not laying again the foundation of repentance from dead works, and of faith toward God.

Hebrews 6:1

Let us draw near with a true heart in full assurance of faith, having our hearts sprinkled from an evil conscience, and our bodies washed with pure water.

Let us hold fast the profession of our faith without wavering; (for he is faithful that promised).

Hebrews 10:22,23

Let us do all we can to help one anther's faith, and this the more earnestly as we see the final day drawing nearer.

Hebrews 10:25b
J. B. Phillips Translation

Cast not away therefore your confidence, which hath great recompence of reward.

For ye have need of patience, that, after ye have done the will of God, ye might receive the promise.

Hebrews 10.35,36

Now the just shall live by faith: but if any man draw back, my soul shall have no pleasure in him.

But we are not of them who draw back unto perdition; but of them that believe to the saving of the soul.

Hebrews 10:38,39

But my righteous one shall live by faith; and if he shrink back, my soul hath no pleasure in him.

Hebrews 10:38
J.B. Phillips Translation

Now faith is being sure of what we hope for and certain of what we do not see. This is what the ancients were commended for.

By faith we understand that the universe was formed at God's command, so that what is seen was not made out of what was visible.

By faith Abel offered God a better sacrifice than Cain did. By faith he was commended as a righteous man, when God spoke well of his offerings. And by faith he still speaks, even though he is dead.

By faith Enoch was taken from this life, so that he did not experience death; he could not be found, because God had taken him away. For before he was taken, he was commended as one who pleased God.

And without faith it is impossible to please God, because anyone who comes to him must believe that he exists and that he rewards those who earnestly seek him.

Hebrews 11:1-6 NIV

By faith Noah, when warned about things not yet seen, in holy fear built an ark to save his family.

By his faith he condemned the world and became heir of the righteousness that comes by faith.

By faith Abraham, when called to go to a place he would later receive as his inheritance, obeyed and went, even though he did not know where he was going. By faith he made his home in the promised land like a stranger in a foreign country, he lived in tents, as did Isaac and Jacob, who were heirs with him of the same promise. For he was looking forward to the city with foundations, whose architect and builder is God.

By faith Abraham, even though he was past age—and Sarah herself was barren—was enabled to become a father because he considered him faithful who had made the promise. And so from this one man, and he as good as dead, came descendants as numerous as the stars in the sky and as countless as the sand on the seashore.

All these people were still living by faith when they died.

Hebrews 11:7-13a NIV

By faith Abraham, when God tested him, offered Isaac as a sacrifice. He who had received the promises was about to sacrifice his one and only son, even though God had said to him, "It is through Isaac that your offspring will be reckoned." Abraham reasoned that God could raise the dead, and figuratively speaking, he did receive Isaac back from death.

By faith Isaac blessed Jacob and Esau in regard to their future.

By faith Jacob, when he was dying, blessed each of Joseph's sons, and worshiped as he leaned on the top of his staff.

By faith Joseph, when his end was near, spoke about the exodus of the Israelites from Egypt and gave instructions about his bones.

By faith Moses' parents hid him for three months after he was born, because they saw he was no ordinary child, and they were not afraid of the king's edict.

By faith Moses, when he had grown up, refused to be known as the son of Pharaoh's daughter.

He chose to be mistreated along with the people of God rather than to enjoy the pleasures of sin for a short time.

He regarded disgrace for the sake of Christ as of greater value than the treasures of Egypt, because he was looking ahead to his reward.

By faith he left Egypt, not fearing the king's anger, he persevered because he saw him who is invisible.

By faith he kept the Passover and the sprinkling of blood, so that the destroyer of the firstborn would not touch the firstborn of Israel.

By faith the people passed through the Red Sea as on dry land; but when the Egyptians tried to do so, they were drowned.

By faith the walls of Jericho fell, after the people had marched around them for seven days.

By faith the prostitute Rahab, because she welcomed the spies, was not killed with those who were disobedient.

Hebrews 11:17-31 NIV

Since we have such a huge crowd of men of faith watching us from the grandstands, let us strip off anything that slows us down or holds us back, and especially those sins that wrap themselves so tightly around our feet and trip us up; and let us run with patience the particular race that God has set before us.

Keep your eyes on Jesus, our leader and instructor. He was willing to die a shameful death on the cross because of the joy he knew would be his afterwards; and now he sits in the place of honor by the throne of God.

If you want to keep from becoming fainthearted and weary, think about his patience as sinful men did such terrible things to him.

Hebrews 12:1-3 TLB

Seeing, therefore, that there is on every side of us such a throng of witnesses, let us also lay aside everything that hinders us, and the sin that clings about us, and run with patient endurance the race that lies before us, our eyes fixed upon Jesus, the Leader and perfect Example of our faith, who, for the joy that lay before him, endured the cross, heedless of its shame, and now "has taken his seat at the right hand" of the throne of God.

Weigh well the example of him who had to endure such opposition from "men who were sinning against themselves," so that you should not grow weary or fainthearted.

Hebrews 12:1-3
The Twentieth Century
New Testament

My brethren, count it all joy when ye fall into divers temptations;

Knowing this, that the trying of your faith worketh patience.

But let patience have her perfect work, that ye may be perfect and entire, wanting nothing.

James 1:2-4

If any of you lack wisdom, let him ask of God, that giveth to all men liberally, and upbraideth not; and it shall be given him.

But let him ask in faith, nothing wavering. For he that wavereth is like a wave of the sea driven with the wind and tossed.

For let not that man think that he shall receive any thing of the Lord.

A double minded man is unstable in all his ways.

James 1:5-8

Dear brothers, what's the use of saying that you have faith and are Christians if you aren't proving it by helping others? Will that kind of faith save anyone? If you have a friend who is in need of food and clothing, and you say to him, "Well, goodbye and God bless you; stay warm and eat hearty," and then don't give him clothes or food, what good does that do?

So you see, it isn't enough just to have faith. You must also do good to prove that you have it. Faith that doesn't show itself by good works is no faith at all—it is dead and useless.

But someone may well argue, "You say the way to God is by faith alone, plus nothing; well, I say that good works are important too, for without good works you can't prove whether you have faith or not; but anyone can see that I have faith by the way I act."

Are there still some among you who hold that "only believing" is enough? Believing in one God? Well, remember that the demons believe this too — so strongly that they tremble in terror! . . . Faith that does not result in good deeds is not real faith.

James 2:14-20b TLB

And the prayer of faith shall save the sick, and the Lord shall raise him up; and if he hath committed sins, they shall be forgiven him.

James 5:15

Blessed be the God and Father of our Lord Jesus Christ, who according to His abundant mercy has begotten us again to a living hope through the resurrection of Jesus Christ from the dead,

To an inheritance incorruptible and undefiled and that does not fade away, reserved in heaven for you,

Who are kept by the power of God through faith for salvation ready to be revealed in the last time.

In this you greatly rejoice, though now for a little while, if need be, you have been grieved by various trials,

That the genuineness of your faith, being much more precious than gold that perishes, though it is tested by fire, may be found to praise, honor and glory at the revelation of Jesus Christ,

Whom having not seen you love. Though now you do not see Him, yet believing, you rejoice with joy inexpressible and full of glory,

Receiving the end of your faith—the salvation of your souls.

1 Peter 1:3-9 NKJV

To those who through the righteousness of our God and Savior Jesus Christ have received a faith as precious as ours;

Grace and peace be yours in abundance through the knowledge of God and of Jesus our Lord.

His divine power has given us everything we need for life and godliness through our knowledge of him who called us by his own glory and goodness. Through these he has given us his very great and precious promises, so that through them you may participate in the divine nature and escape the corruption in the world caused by evil desires.

For this reason, make every effort to add to your faith goodness; and to goodness, knowledge; and to knowledge, selfcontrol; and to self-control, perseverance; and to perseverance, godliness; and to godliness, brotherly kindness; and to brotherly kindness, love. For if you possess these qualities in increasing measure, they will keep you from being ineffective and unproductive in your knowledge of our Lord Jesus Christ. But if anyone does not have them, he is nearsighted and blind, and has forgotten that he has been cleansed from his past sins.

Therefore, my brothers, be all the more eager to make your calling and election sure. For if you do these things, you will never fall.

2 Peter 1:1b-10 NIV

For whatever is born of God overcomes the world; and this is the victory that has overcome the world—our faith.

And who is the one who overcomes the world, but he who believes that Jesus is the Son of God.

1 John 5:4,5 NASB

These things I have written to you who believe in the name of the Son of God, in order that you may know that you have eternal life.

And this is the confidence which we have before Him, that, if we ask anything according to His will, He hears us.

And if we know that He hears us in whatever we ask, we know that we have the requests which we have asked from Him.

1 John 5:13-15 NASB

But you, beloved, building yourselves up on your most holy faith, praying in the Holy Spirit,

Keep yourselves in the love of God, looking for the mercy of our Lord Jesus Christ unto eternal life.

Jude 20,21 NKJV

But do you, dear friends, build up your characters on the foundation of your most holy Faith, pray under the guidance of the Holy Spirit, and keep within the love of God, while waiting for the mercy of our Lord Jesus Christ, to bring you to Immortal Life?

Jude 20,21
The Twentieth Century
New Testament

References

Scripture quotations marked AMP are taken from *The Amplified Bible, Old Testament,* copyright © 1965, 1987 by The Zondervan Corporation, Grand Rapids, Michigan, or *The Amplified Bible, New Testament,* copyright © 1958, 1987 by The Lockman Foundation, La Habra, California. Used by permission.

Verses marked TLB are taken from *The Living Bible* © 1971. Used by permission of Tyndale House Publishers, Inc., Wheaton, Illinois 60189. All rights reserved.

Scripture quotations marked *Moffatt's Translation* are taken from *The Bible, James Moffatt Translation,* copyright © 1922, 1924, 1925, 1926, 1935 by Harper Collins San Francisco; copyright © 1950, 1952, 1953, 1954 by James A. R. Moffatt; and copyright © 1994 by Kregel Publications, Grand Rapids, Michigan.

Scripture quotations marked NASB are taken from the *New American Standard Bible,* copyright © 1960, 1962, 1963, 1968, 1971, 1972, 1973, 1975, 1977 by The Lockman Foundation, La Habra, California.

Scripture quotations marked NKJV are taken from the *New King James Version.* Copyright © 1979, 1980, 1982, Thomas Nelson, Inc.

Some Scripture quotations marked NIV are taken from *The Holy Bible, New International Version*®. NIV®. Copyright © 1973, 1978, 1984 by International Bible Society. Used

Prayer of Salvation

God loves you—no matter who you are, no matter what your past. God loves you so much that He gave His one and only begotten Son for you. The Bible tells us that "...whoever believes in him shall not perish but have eternal life" (John 3:16 NIV). Jesus laid down His life and rose again so that we could spend eternity with Him in heaven and experience His absolute best on earth. If you would like to receive Jesus into your life, say the following prayer out loud and mean it from your heart.

Heavenly Father, I come to You admitting that I am a sinner. Right now, I choose to turn away from sin, and I ask You to cleanse me of all unrighteousness. I believe that Your Son, Jesus, died on the cross to take away my sins. I also believe that He rose again from the dead so that I might be forgiven of my sins and made righteous through faith in Him. I call upon the name of Jesus Christ to be the Savior and Lord of my life. Jesus, I choose to follow You and ask that You fill me with the power of the Holy Spirit. I declare that right now I am a child of God. I am free from sin and full of the righteousness of God. I am saved in Jesus' name. Amen.

If you prayed this prayer to receive Jesus Christ as your Savior for the first time, please contact us on the web at www.harrisonhouse.com to receive a free book.

Or you may write to us at
Harrison House
P.O. Box 35035
Tulsa, Oklahoma 74153

Other Harrison House Pocket Bibles

The Pocket Bible on Protection
The Pocket Bible on Healing
The Pocket Bible on Finances

Available from your
local bookstore.

If this book has been a blessing to you
or if you would like to see more of
the Harrison House product line,
please visit us on our website at
<u>www.harrisonhouse.com</u>

Harrison House
Tulsa, OK 74153

The Harrison House Vision

Proclaiming the truth and the power
Of the Gospel of Jesus Christ
With excellence;

Challenging Christians to
Live victoriously,
Grow spiritually,
Know God intimately.